Moleskine #3:
33 Extra Poems

colvet

All poems written by Colvet in Hamilton, ON and Cleveland, OH sometime between 2018-2019, except for American Crow #1 written in 2020.

Cover art is a close-up of an original painting done by the author using spray and acrylic paint entitled "Hamilton #1", the first installment of a mixed media project focusing on "fine art" abstractions on pieces of wood/debris found in the city streets. See www.colvet.net for more if interested.

◈ ◈ ◈

Published D.I.Y. in Feb. 2021 via Amazon KDP.

Please note that the first two books in the Moleskine series were created using the re-flowable option on Amazon KDP to auto-detect chapter titles, which was never a perfect process. I selected to publish this one as a .pdf copy of the raw poems. Your feedback on the change is appreciated.

Moleskine #3: 33 Extra Poems
1. Collapsed, finally
2. Sunshine
3. Past lives hash pipe (something at least)
4. They call it
5. Diodes
6. Newlows new lows NL
7. Yellow cut roses
8. An aerosolizing life
9. Airbus ascending
10. Dreamworks
11. Random Thought
12. 27 bones
13. My hand wrote this, my hand scares me I
14. My hand wrote this, my hand scares me II
15. City bus (self-election)
16. Conversation with Self Vol. I
17. Mulberry Thoughts – projection///ownership
18. Halloween Twenty Nineteen
19. Motion Controller
20. Special Dose
21. Integration Day (first day of snow)
22. Yelling-Men-Made Trauma Deposits
23. Shadow Daemon
24. No Ragerts
25. Dual Worlds
26. To the Lady in the Black Overcoat
27. Home
28. Xenodonut
29. Excalibur [a technological intuition]
30. To do list #1
31. [set]tle
32. American Crow #1
33. Long shot, one shot, one kill, head shot

Collapsed, finally

you make some stunning
riveting
realizations
the moment you span the room
redefined as a basement apartment
to grab your therapist's business card
to fold up like an accordion
get that "W" or "M" always sought
to serve as a measly filter
for your rolled up
drug salad
synergy of neurotopic effects

said realizations
simply tell you
to get your shit together
and grow the fuck up
but the pain of roaming this planet
alone
one more day
brings you in
pulls you closer
for another pull of drugs
into your damp and dark
smoker lungs
collapsed,
---
finally

…end…

Sunshine

Some days
I buy multiple coffee cups
even if I don't need the caffeine boost
just to hear
the lovely library laboring ladies
call me sunshine
and tell me to have a great day
I am so pathetic
and meek

...end...

Past lives hash pipe
(something at least)

grabbing the hash pipe
immediately thinking
alone in bed
of smoking tetrahydrocannabinol crystals
shiny minty crystals
as I blow smoke
in the evergreen
crawling English Ivy
cramped crawlspace patio
but enjoyable
nonetheless
pipe bowls
keep billowing smoke
to get inspiration
or something at least

but having a thought
of pure brilliance
of poetic beauty charm
anxiety side effects
leave mind left drifting
a stumble
and a sway
so subtle
yet reminiscent
of the scars you painted my skin with
and the degeneration my body language leaves

best they are put on me
so cunning

and dashing
and destructive
in your psychopathic ways
still popping off
in my brainwaves
every once in awhile
so sweet
so manipulative
and vile
I digress

See
he scarred me
but I still love back
and absorb water
like the Morton salt girl
dumping heaves of salted crack
on the sidewalk
to prevent snow accumulation
drug clearly crystallized
bubbling off now

but I am much better alone
watching current life
becomes much simpler
past lives
past energy
past consciousness
is still
at the end of the day
just potential
and kinetic energy
all must be conserved

$$\Delta KE = \Delta PE = 0$$

So basically
I was a bum
a hobo
in my past life
or one of them at least
I hopped trains
I was free
I was me

This person has come out
of the wood working shop
and has taken hold of me
writing this now
and he's still nothing
but alone
but free
and he rides around
respects others
never wants to be a bother
is paranoid of the watching eyes

an aloof
open-minded
creative
intelligent
adaptive
orator
circumnavigator
brain stormer
traveler
free individual

it is getting harder and harder to be one
in 2019
but alas
we wander
we roam
and maybe
Madeleine is right
green is not the best colour
east is not the best coast

rather -
aim for golden
high as you can go
golden sands
golden beaches
golden dreams
I never had enough courage
to allow myself to deserve rarity

I'll ride freight
all the way
to the golden states
to get my creative
inner potential power
away from you
by shifting my kinetic mass flux
to find someone else
or something that matters
at least

...end...

They call it
my big black book
holds all the secrets
to the scribing hand
called the soul
but your gaze
may never skip along
the pages
dance across
the curved sketched lines
"your smile is the best piece of art you've ever
made"
still blighting
the neural network
called the brain
my work never aimed to please
my suffering never sought to ease
but creation
the very process
is what both
soul and brain
need

…end…

Diodes

diodes blinking
down a long cylindrical spiral
stuffed in the confines of your mouth
an effervescent ectoplasm
luminous afterglow effect
I'd rather -
read the contents of your soul
from the intensity
of light dripping
from your salivary glands
than sift through the rubble
lost in sand
as it protrudes out
of your porous eggnog coated teeth
like a sputtering spout
in an abandoned
Midwestern shopping mall complex boutique
power lines still hot
never let the light
of your diodes go out

...end...

Newlows new lows NL

observations
are best made
whilst wobbly wandering
the local cityscape playground
"Happy first day of JK Chris"
first catches a glance
another happenstance
"Happy first day of school"
I read
as I wave the back of my hand
across the curvature of my mouth
to prevent
the hyperemetic
surge of bile
my stomach is aimlessly trying
to churn out
leaving a rancid reminder
of the bag of hot chips
two, no four tall cans
and spit-diluted
crack-coated cigarette
the street-folk of Detroit
rock city
left my body
to simply sit with
I'll heave and moan
and choke
on chunkified puke
in my luke-warm
seafoam green painted bathtub
each pulsation

and violent purge
of an empty de-detoxifying gut
will leave me
craving boiled lemon water
because the heat
helps open up your vocal chords
as the viscous
pre-digested
meal of artificial colours
splashes
on the antiquated squishy
matching seafoam green
toilet seat
Fuck this
new low achieved

NL
NL
NL

…end…

Yellow cut roses

even in earnest days
of an earned PhD
my lighters
set flowers ablaze
almost every single day
but today
most definitely
I breathe botanical death
on my trek into the office
glassbox rat cage
so the cut roses left
for the awardee not present
or left for decorum
will get a sprinkle of urine

sometimes nature's beauty
runs more deep
bends more barriers
of what we can perceive
now every time
you smell yellow roses
please think
of me,
no,
of pee

…end…

An aerosolizing life

The problem lies
when people lie
and sit
in silence
harrumphing
with vulnerability
inside
pouring out
of their pores
and into
their aerosolized life
we take in
and breathe out
smoker lung
cough
bloody phlegm
shooting pain
down arm and side
and let it wisp
past their rotting teeth
into the air
we also breathe
filtration needed

…end…

Airbus ascending

I have heard
or have read in a book somewhere
that if you crack your back
at the perfect sweet spot
upon the ascent
of an airborne A321 air bus
one may actually
cut off their central
and peripheral
nervous systems
from the surrounding tissues
exudation of all my nervousness
may be the long-sought solution
to me attempting anxiety reduction
I'd rather pay the $200
for my one-way
stand-by
flight
than live one more day
in this grueling
grinding
grandiose
simulation
of life

...end...

Dreamworks

Celestial tidings
guided by a crescent moon
dripping fog
into the ethereal void of nothingness
of consciousness
we collectively deem
as air

All the mushrooms
fungi and molds
exploiting the gloominous
hygroscopic forest floor
flooring to some
ostentatious to all

Raindrops patter
off the abandoned hospital clinic
banging
on the rusty metal housing overhang
pinging
down dusty window panes unwashed
creating a mosaic
art installment
left to dry
on the lonely concrete floor

How can life's elixir
bear so much calmness//uniqueness
and utter destruction
simultaneously?

Our inner Dreamworks
are constantly in progress

…end…

Random Thought

Grown men
with
hairless
legs
utterly
scare
and deter
me.

…end…

27 bones

At twenty-seven
my bones (and their containing)
joints and ligaments
connectors

seem to creak more
than a dungeon door

seem to cavitate in order
louder than bubbles in silicone oil

seem to still contain flexural strength
like an aged anodized steel beam

seem to bacterially decay
similar to brothy brine-riddled wooden posts

seem to become infinitely more porous
like your osteoarthritic grandma Doris

seem to get duller and more morose
like the skin of an avid addict with a special
dose

But still
you hold me up
hips bearing the weight inside
so I guess I can't complain
I'll continue to crack
every 10-15 minutes
still inside

noises permeating out
grotesque head-turning fun

...end...

My hand wrote this, my hand scares me I

so hey, I'm M------
I have BPD
well traits officially is what I should tell others
but full-blown
mild of course
but worsening still
anyways

I told my mom on messenger
in the midst of a full blown
emotionally overloaded episode
after cancelling plans
with newfound friends
after searching and searching
and finding
told her I have seven
yes seven
demons in my head

Didn't really know what I meant
but said it anyways
I logged off
will talk again in the AM
and walked to the corner's
abandoned parking lot
dimly lit
tree dense zoo
upon cylindrical concrete pillars
to get high
because it "shuts the demons up"

or so I claimed
but it really just brought one more out
See, let me explain:

Seven
1. motherly figure
2. authoritative egoist
3. critical self
4. punk/teenage angster
5. lover and dreamer duo
6. philosophical hobo
7. "cool" guy and "creative" guy duo

they all guide me
tug at me
at the same damn time
it works like this...
I've been broken
from birth
emotionally sensitive
intellectually advanced
high IQ
off the chart's emotions
so my parents

loving mom with bad anxiety and regret

plus

authoritative power-hungry metrosexual betta
boy

yields

invalidated child
because parents cannot understand
whipping ideas in head
constant mental images and thoughts
cathartic pain
vulnerability
chronic fright

so it created a broken individual
so much emotional sensitivity
so much brain processing
wasted
into sorrowful skim milk tears
alone
smoking in the woods again
to feel something
even chest pain
or head rush bubbling
so what did I do?

I mirrored those around me
who raised me
who inspired me
who shaped me
I've developed seven so far
I'm so scared
of how many unknowing fuckers
will stick to my shirt
latch with their circular jaws
and enter into me
woven and wandering
into my bloodstream

so basically
I see people
and I mirror them
but none are attached
so I feel
like it is more of a magic trick

(visualize seven mirrors in a circle and a
hologram of a boy in middle)

So
when meeting people
they see the hologram
it's me
well or how I appear
they hear all of them
come out and alive
see their figures form
bodies bust
from their mirrored
illusioned
apartments
into living life

That's why everyone calls me an "enigma"
fuck that word
but you know
not normal
to meet a BPD metal-head stoner PhD engineer
poet writer artist vandal international gaming
…wandering alien
left and right brained?

weird
an empath?
more like sociopath

so anyways
everyone always figures the trick out
maybe
that's why I always go for dumb boys
so eventually
everyone leaves
its just a matter
of how much time does it take
to clear all the dusty gunk
from their eyes
and see the trick
for who M------ really was
or is
or is not

and this puts
the biggest sensation
of that
[rollercoaster shitty losing your innards feeling
upon descent but then it kind of gets better once
you hit free fall]
into my gut

When does that feeling end for me?
it keeps going on and on
day by day
and my black pit
disorderly-fed stomach
can't handle its churning anymore

Let me jump the bridge
and free fall

…end…

My hand wrote this, my hand scares me II

So I've thought harder
getting high
same spot as before
so I thought
with these personalities
Blair (therapist/counselor)
kind of corroborated their presence
our shadow selves
Jungian archetypes
very interesting topic
will learn more
his techniques
of grounding
have helped
massively
anyways
I thought
of the seven
the ones mapped out
in the aside
adjacent page in my moleskine
I thought
can the seven ever interact?
some clearly adore
even look up to others
some despise
think waste of time of others
so in the end
they must interact
Go back to the mirror image/vision

what would the projection
hologram
as I bolster
of M------
look like
if two were talking
chatting
gaining
life-changing platonic moments
I very much desire?
I pictured this
take a red ball
and then a blue ball
hold each up
individually
to one
singular mirror
the red...
appears red and sphere
the blue...
appears blue and sphere
now...
hold both up, simultaneously
one in each hand like 40 oz.
close
not touching
to the same mirror
will they look
the same as before?
or as an amalgamation
of half red sphere plus half blue sphere?
so the projection is different
changed

my point....
what is my "current"
personality?
How do I describe it?
How does its borosilicate reflection appear?
I picture this interaction:

A. creative guy
> wants to....
- create art
- watch art Youtube videos
- go to galleries and museums
- Hamilton Shitcrawl
- view murals
- see live music/shows

< < < picture "red ball" > > >

plus

B. punk/teenage angster
> wants to...
- trainhop
- wheatpaste
- graff
- poetically justify
- be a mental health activist or patient?

,< < < picture "blue ball" > > >

yields

"the writer"

the cultural jammer of ideologies and creation
big old number eight
but he is more of a "side interaction"
only when both punk and creative interact
half red sphere, half blue sphere

that's who I am
social outcast
isolation tendency
substance abuse
black hate
acceptance of death
willing to risk
to feel
to express
to write
and to be

...end...

City bus (self-election)

city spanning
city bus ride
out to east end
hoping
just hoping
they will accept
my rain-soaked
dampened
"free pizza for a year"
coupon card
stag and doe
awardee
not present
hammy down charity
from a local hero
preparing
just preparing
for rain-soaked
shoes and socks
for the hour walk home
trials and tribulations
of a mental patient's
self-elected
day off

...end...

Conversation with Self
Vol. I

the pain
is so intense
in my chest
as I cup
my large coffee A & W cup
between my fat-devoid thighs
the boy I've met online
who has seen
my most vulnerable self
yet real words
real interactions
in the "real" world
have not yet been established
body boiling in heat
on a late September morning
we only sat
for a single stop
he obviously knew
to walk straight
to the back of the bus
it makes your anxiety
so apparent
like I'm a psychologist
treating a patient
residing within me
He's so weak
the boy could have left
because his friend is in the back
or to free up room
for priority seating

blind seeing eye dog
handicapped
physical injury
pregnant
nope
none on this shuttle
But alas --
he is conversing
so smoothly
so effortlessly
I need to stop
projecting my fears of myself
and my doubts
of responsibility and purpose
in this purposeful life
a sudden pull
an inertia burning
staining
the inside of my TV static jeans
worn since 9th grade or before
it reminds you
that all clothes
stain the same
all bodies bruise alike
and all psyches
can get swept up
by the gushing waves of insecurity
.
..
...
But I am not the best at swimming
skills a bit rusty
also

my lungs
get tired sometimes.
.::agape::.

...end...

Mulberry Thoughts – projection///ownership

People in life
really need to take hold
of their own stories
if you think about it
we are all only guided by stories

some told by riveting orators
so we believe
even into adulthood
even if ignorant or misguided
insert flat earth or any other bogus belief

some only ever see one perspective
their angles or vision never tested
living in or out of the cave
thus becomes pure black and white

we cannot expect
our stories
to always line up like the stars
or have the same plot
characters
verbiage
language
rising/fall action
climax
meaning
etc.

to end karmic/re-forming hate

we don't need either side
each soap box orator
to increase their volume or timbre
or to become more violent
rather ---
realize we are all independent authors

some may have
the same ghost-writing buddies
but the first author
final printed name
is unique
so why are we expecting horror writers
to work in the realm of history?
or vice versa?
we cannot all know everything
or know all meaning
the only truth

back to mental health
we all have own our story
our own experience
but some people live
in so much disgust
so much trauma
their vision is occluded with offenses

they truly believe
that everyone
yes, every single one
must accommodate their triggers
walk around them
avoid them

or understand them so intimately
past the point of decency
seems exhausting

but end of the day
you cannot project your traumas
your dark parts
shadow selves if you like Jung
and expect everyone
even people
who don't know your middle fucking name
to know how to act
or deal with your demons
that is not our role
that is not time well spent

we all
must wake up
and swallow that huge gelatinous pill
we cannot keep projecting
our shadow selves
onto others
without scaring them
those demon faces are wicked and grueling
and expect them
to muster up the courage
and help us engage in the fight

make your story yours
a printed novel
not a Wikipedia page
editable by any fucking person
after you publish

maybe the world wont appear so
...
...end...

Halloween Twenty Nineteen

writing in the dark
just got home
glasses still drippy
rain-soaked
putting on
chill, relaxing vibes
met a boy
17 year old
trick or treater
approached me
in a white mask
pillowcase billowing
with candy treats
he asked
"you smoke weed?"
he saw me
wiping the residual
oil pastel markings
from the rain ghosted
rusto-bars
train track view
saw me
standing hooded
smoking flowers
and asked
"you smoke weed?"
a reply in agreeance
I approach
agape flow
demon eyes bugged

suppressed
hand is scribbling in pain
back of brain
seriously hurting now
we talk
of many things
graffiti - he wants in
interested
my mentee, ha
actually though
but he told me two riveting tales
< < < one > > >
did an acid trip
room transitioned
into a dungeon
lamp = torch
outside pond = moat
shingles = laden brick
wall = casteled
I was in awe
said it lasted 10 minutes
then all return back to calm
I like that
0.5 g
wait 30 minutes or if no effect
1.0 g more
nice
< < < two > > >
was skating
oh yeah he skates
taught him some shit
a thing or two from my days
he's seen my tag

knows my real name
fuck
ah well
he's 17
smoking weed
illegal
I'm ok
second story still
< 2 >
was skating at city hall
with some buds
saw a guy
placed in a Muskoka chair
with a sign stating "KING"
they are intrigued
they are 17
they are smoking
they are skating
city hall
Kirkendall
asking
that same riveting question
so familiar now
"you smoke weed?"
kids, eh
he said, "hell yes"
they smoke together
3 people
1 joint
after some neurosis
psychosis
and neural apoptosis
the man

starts to explain
explaining
that he is a messenger of Satan
he would interrupt his own speech
to speak in tongues
black fucking metal
straight to the devil
and ask
"who is the devil?"
"who is he?"
the boys rightfully got the fuck out of there
the guy was cool
seriously forget his name
my boots weren't even tied
but wrote down my name
in his phone
has no SIM card like me
he will make an account
just to talk to me
humbling
a fist bump
a smile
a parting of ways
in only the three minute walk home
BAM
Idea
next two galleries
illegible word(s?)
intuition
to new friend made
and a cramped hand
the galleries:
/ / / one \ \ \

paint
my interpretation
of other people's acid
drug-induced
mental trips

/ / / two \ \ \
do
the same drugs
paint what my eye
and soul
see

…

power
literally just went out
around 11 PM
went out for a smoke
crazy rain
come back in
debating to knock
hear a beep
shine flashing light down the stairs
confusion
flash off
power back on?
spooked
so spooked
Halloween
Twenty
Nine
Teen

…end…

Motion controller

first one into the office
fuck these motion-controlled lights
morning coffees in darkness are not so bad

last one in the office to leave
fuck these motion-controlled lights
I just want to finish this paper and take a nap

…end…

Special Dose

we are all searching
yearning
for our special dose
writing this now
from memory
moments left
for mind
be wandering
writing less frantic
ideas intact nonetheless
maybe less poetic
but I digress
inner critic at rest
but mental health patients
know this more than any
the special dose
so cryptic
unbeknownst
yet the treasure
in our sleep deprived
goop glistening eyes
well I watched a film
surrounding addiction
with Madeleine
Saturday night theater
was stunning
every scene
every piece of art
dangling on set walls
and the moment
you become slaved

imprisoned
i.e. drugs
it leaves you broken
and empty
and sorrowful
since part is of your own doing
mind over matter
more truth within
than science sheds light on
you need inspiration
passion
meaning
you must look
and analyze
all parts
of your fragmented hard-drive
and painstakingly
strive for hours
to code the correct prompt
to glue all the puzzle pieces
back together
it's formulation
nutrition facts
on the backside of the packaging
first ingredient/additive
special dose 47 - SD47
it may have taken
46 failed bench-scale
grad student slaved
experimental attempts
some helped mildly
others bear hallucinogenic side effects
but that number 47

wow
does it really have great
effectiveness
efficiency
efficacy
effluence...
we all need to be open
to those failed trials
look at what was missing
honestly
and in what quantity
to yield the best
phenotypic response
I've had failed trials
experiments
in my technical field
and otherwise
for mental health
as is the best/most relatable
herein
a sudden scratch
in my right side
my abdomen
what the hell?
reddened now
and tingling
going to try to ignore
and continue
maybe
ok
coffee first
its small
calm

fine
good
yup
ok
but yeah
I've failed
11 years straight
11 fucking years
all SSRIs under the sun
new SNRIs
mild improvement for anxiety
side effects too great
microdosed psilocybin
amazing
hard to buy
illegal
olanzapine
lithium
klonopin
anti-anxieties
CBT
DBT
etc.
etc.
etc.
new therapist
has a soul
understands
and feels
he gets universal vibrations
he understands
I'm searching for SD47
so I can have

the only side effect
of cathartically vomiting
the contents of my soul
into the void of the universe
for wanderers and travelers
to gaze upon
interact with
and connect to my soul with
anonymously
yet still emotionally real
I think I finally
finally
discovered my special dose
let's call it SD28 for now
my age
who knows how long it will last
don't want to get too excited
but our one-on-one therapy
talks of shadow selves
Carl Jung
queer resilience
trauma unraveling
emotional integration
Shamanic/spiritual grounding
philosophical talks
anatomy re-caps
intellectual stimulation
sharing of poems/expression
real fucking therapy
actual effective therapy
plus
the integration
of my path/journey

into my expressions
poems
visual arts
mind wanders
it has integrated my soul
de-fragmented my hard-drive
hand writing calm
I must be nearing the end
of this jazzy riff
but now my art
may terrify me
but it motivates me
pushes me
to push these shadow selves
inner demons
trauma scars
imaginary paranoias
dreams
imaginations
and hallucinations
into gallery lights
splayed on canvas
and wooden panels
or stuck in some case
this project
my art
has integrated
my soul
into my every physical fiber
of my very being
so now
being
is not

as scary
and never
as alone.

11:33 AM - 2019-11-10
...end...

Integration Day (first day of snow)

Monday afternoon
integration day
hand still numbingly cold
writing slow
hoodie bundled
after therapy
head to back end
medical centre side
of campus
have a smoke
wait for bus
but decide to walk
to busier terminal
better chance
of having my 30+ min
expired transfer ticket
accepted
in exchange
for a cramped lift home
back of the bus
witness a woman
crying
bobbing
her black jean covered knee
up///down///up
like a DIY tattoo gun
notice another gentleman
offer her his coffee cup
to warm her hands
poor thing misunderstood

at least he's helping
I'm just sitting here
feeling bad
already missed my stop
well to home at least
have many possible ideas
places
to explore
sketchbook and pens in bag
notice her getting ready
to leave
ask her simply
for her name
possibly to divert
that cricused mind
she responds
I ask
stupidly
"Having a rough day?"
"Anxiety?"
"Want to talk?"
Just like how
she returned the coffee cup
to its rightful owner
with a
"Here -
I'm afraid I'll accidentally take your drink"
deflecting blame
onto herself
willingly
so when it is her fault
really
its not as big of a shock

common tactic of mine
brethren in arms
she replied to me
"Oh I don't want to take up too much of your
time."
I explain
"Oh, I have nowhere to be,
I passed my house 4 (over-exaggeration) stops
ago"
< she chokes up >
we agree
to depart at MacNab bus terminal
together
fetch a Timmies
chat
as we do
whilst finding
where to sit
she asks
"fair a smoke?"
interestingly phrased
nodding in agreeance
we speak
and share
on many things
hateful exs
artistic drives
mental debilitation
similar symptoms
life
to which
she was posing
life itself

an intriguing question
rhetorical still
but to why
pwBPD
live as though
they have a bright neon sign
like at a nail salon
wedged into their scalp
saying something
to the degree of
"walk all over me"
"DUMBO"
"Treat me like shit"
"Abuse me"
"Make my life living hell"
"Love me"
right before I asked
if she ever followed her intuition
ever listened to her soul
she agrees
citing situations
of other-worldly-led-writing
late night endeavors
I say yes
I feel this
very much so
in my own art
and writing
right at this time
a pudgy
red and angry man
leaves the shopping centre
yelling

in utter disgust
he approaches near us
severing
the agape cord
stretching between our auras
taking up
my new friend's
frozen coffee
which I purchased
with $10 free in world
and says
some FUCKED SHIT
about how "they"
call me a garbage man
I'm waste disposal
fuck you
watch
I don't care
I'll do shit
and smashes
her entire drink
on the snow and piss covered sidewalk
and the tagged metal trashcan
I'm instantly angered
say to my new friend
in such a frenzy rage
I don't care if I'm skinny
this dude fucking sucks
hatred spins in circles
you've never learned this
me neither
hence the shitty occurrences
that keep finding us

so I fight back
verbal word sauce stew
dude is angered
I back down
logic of new friend
"dude's a wacko"
unstable
so I stop
I did
He walks away
we relax
finish our secondary smokes
freezing cold
unprepared
he returns
speaks in tongues at use
eyes rolled back
and then runs
I ask her...
"Ever hear of synchronicities?"
She says
"No, sounds cool though"
to which I reply
"look it up,
follow your gut,
think of what just happened"
we walk back
to the train station
origin point
thru mall warm
shortcut
a hug
an exchange of names

a meltdown averted
a new soul healing/emerging
agape

Colvet 2019-11-11
...end...

Yelling-Men-Made Trauma Deposits

heart
compelled to write
as I cough out remnant smoke
interesting
the way he knows
the three special spots
regions of interest
which are tightened
hardened
pained
in my crooked spinal cord
pain figuratively
literally
were caused
from the empty deposits of you
called trauma
left within me still
body not recognized
as foreign yet
once depressed
cracked
popped
a gush of bright red blood
lost to the crevices
of my internal transverse plane
filling new spots
with heme and life
purity in some sense
maybe it targets
the same spots

recently dug up
archaeologically sound
via therapeutic means
and gives them
the red liquid payload
the same part
gluing back
your micro-crack propagated
sense of consciousness
forcing you to state
"you remind me of my father"
yelling men make me uncomfortable
yelling men make me recall
yelling men make me yell
stop yelling about slow traffic
and lulling pedestrians in crosswalks
just follow the flow
get it?

…end…

Shadow Daemon

after post-work
flower bowls
the porch light
never acknowledges my presence
motion-sensor silenced
yet
when I turn the key
pull the knob
whoever is standing behind me
he
some daemon
looming over every shouldering move
is stark enough to trip the sensor
and dissolve into the surrounding photons of
light
wonder if he is like a vampire
needing an invitation
or pulsating energy
to survive

...end...

No Ragerts

you ask
"ever regret Canada?"
to which I reply
with words sucked
from the void of ambient air
"no"
"the term regret is not part of my vernacular"
I further explain
that hindsight
is never useful
unless you are operating
a moving vehicle

…end…

Dual Worlds

in a world
where prison wardens
line the seams of their pockets
for warmth in winter months
while the PhD
sits
and starves alone
only indulging
on the remnant meat off bone
dangling
from their star-bound mental platter
I don't need justice for all overnight
- - - But a bite
of something freshly green
would certainly be nice

...end...

To the Lady in the Black Overcoat

my inspiration
does not come
from scientists or engineers
who patent data
design new drugs
I'm captivated
by the lady in a black silky overcoat
who drives remote controlled cars around
outside the "as seen on TV" shop
her dedication
and resilience
to keep pushing on
pushes me
to question the sanctity
of my own
self-imposed
reality
paranoid
grounded

…end…

Home

our traumas are
shattered
our memories get
tattered
our histories have become
star-spangled bannered
on this historical landmass
taken for granted, rather
a ball of yarn
spun by the stars
home

…end…

Xenodonut

To live on a ring
high above the stars
en route
to Clouds of Magellan
a frontier of xenophized zones afar
skycycling alone
a post-smash aircraft sits
getting beamed down
a kzin cat bemoans
a seeking solace sought
in heaven
in a city
floating
above the stars
mach 4 numbers needed
to get the ship to float
please lightyears, keep us on par
to reach that pressurized
donut ring
flying with rotating sprinkles
sparkles
splayed colour
cancerous
it seems
growing/glowing
amongst the stars

...end...

Excalibur [a technological intuition]

your fate:
disembowelled & decapitated by a laptop

my role:
to be the one to have to use my hips and knees
for more torque like when you watch washed
out dads start their lawnmowers for the first
time in spring as I have to rip out the Excalibur
laptop deeply cased in the bony crystal cage
once called your skull

take-home message:
technology will kill us all...a clean-cut severing
brain from body

...end...

To do list #1

to do list:
- buy milk

- get eggs

- resupply trash bags

- bomb Asbest, Russia finally since no one else will

- learn how to scale-up a Drano bomb on Youtube

- Convince others that we are actually living in a society where murder is 100% legal as long as there is money to be gained and enough people agree (the number of instances in recorded human history is shocking if you wake up) and that no one is brave enough to do anything about it so their hazardous Russian mining methods and distribution of a cancerous substance will likely just continue happening for another 100 years causing our DNA and cells to rapidly mutate and morph so much so that we may progress evolution to an even greater extent than the surfactants in your deodorant and hygiene products are already doing on a daily basis so that the next "evolution" actually comes sooner than expected in our own lifetimes but it wont be like a frog-human or flying chimera but really a retrograding effect yielding schizoaffective mental and emotional oversurges which prevent us from functionally using this beatific materialistic world we have all strived so hard for with hours of research and investment to create and enjoy over the last hundreds of years, forcing us to isolate ourselves in our homes like a Hikikomori because our faces will be too menacing and our resoluteness of mental capabilities will be so fucked leaving us vulnerable to anything that moves or even things that do not, yet we will continue the "war on drugs" because drugs are bad and fear tactics work, right?

- write a poem

- cry in bed

at least I can cross one of these off my list today...

...end...

[set]tle
The setting sun
will always set
even if
your setting
is unsettling

…end…

American Crow #1

an American crow
fitted with a plump, stocky build
a messenger of death
and a walker among worlds
he who soars
the weightless perimeter
of the sky castle abyss of divination
in the infinite loop of skyward dreams
a simple guttural caw
or the brilliant blue effervescent sheen
from the oily black feathers
exposed to sun-dropped photons
a simple shadow
an image of your outline overhead
peripheral in frame
form perched on the buzzing network above
is enough to halt my cadence
reflect within
and allow a bright emerald green wheel
to begin to churn
take heed guide
for I am forever grateful
for your electric field
for your etheric body
for your astral plane
for your historically-tested insights
serve me in the highest good
for all of those involved
and I'll promise
to do my best to decipher your message
your world which continuously transcends

beyond common geographical or cultural limits
yet not lost in translation
I urge my friends
to never fear your feathers
for the blackness absorbs all wavelengths for us
a spectacular energy sink, life-filled reservoir
Hail and farewell old friend
Agape in the highest
until we meet again

...end...

Long shot, one shot, one kill, head shot

Not skilled enough
to get a man copped
with a long shot
one shot
one kill
head shot
with lasers beaming
across unknowing terrain
empty cartridges rolling
across deserted urban avenues
death in war
is not a sustainable memory
clip your wings
escape through an alternative route

…end…

thanks for being my ride or dies
(**you** reading this now)

I write because I feel like this shit matters
Myself and others need this perspective
This time to reflect
To make sense
To not lose hope
To not forget love

Especially
When we choose to not listen
And blow the entire globe apart
Boom

If you are offended
Or put off from my work
That's ok
Write your own damn book instead
We can never have enough of 'em

But this one
This one right here
This is my dream
My wish
My book
Goonies never say die

...no end...

only
interlocking
loops